THE ALIEN GODS: 10 COMMANDMENTS

PALMETTO
PUBLISHING
Charleston, SC
www.PalmettoPublishing.com

The Alien Gods: 10 Commandments
Copyright © 2024 by Rion Baxter

First Edition

Hardcover ISBN: 979-8-8229-4715-3
Paperback ISBN: 979-8-8229-4716-0
eBook ISBN: 979-8-8229-4717-7

THE ALIEN GODS:

10 COMMANDMENTS

BLUEPRINT TO HEAVEN ON EARTH 360

RION BAXTER

PART 1

ALOHA,

Thank you so much for giving some of your precious time to open and read this book. Everything inside is in accordance with the Laws of Nature and Laws of the Universe. If anything, you read is 'triggering' that is a delightful clue for you to reform a limiting belief you possess.

So here's the story: Us Aliens Gods came down and visited the writer one night, at his farm on the 'Holy' Big Island of Hawaii and told him all the information in this book. We told him to pass it on to humanity by writing a book. You can view him as a messenger or disciple of us Alien Gods. Something Muslims, Hindus, Buddhist, Christians and everyone else can agree on! Unlike other authors who write hundreds of pages and expect you to take hours of your precious time, we tried to keep this as sweet, short, and simple as possible. Get ready for the trip of a lifetime :)

1. Do not kill or hurt each other.
2. Stop creating deadly technology.
3. Create technology to help humanity and Mother Nature
4. Connect with Mother Nature more,
   human technology less.
5. Fair taxes with reasonable wealth distribution.
6. Respect and promote family values. Mother
   and Father in household with children.
7. Maintain 'Divine' Sex to Mother Nature connection.
8. Practice Spiritual Health.
9. Keep children and adults truthful,
   innocent and pure hearted.
10. Understand these Commandments came from God.

1. Do not kill or hurt each other. This one is universal. Absolutely no more wars, no violence, no destruction. Some refer to it as the golden rule, to "treat others the ways you want to be treated." Similarly, the platinum rule is to "treat others the ways they want to be treated." Use your energy to create Love, Health, Peace, and Joy. Eliminate fear, anger, distrust and negativity from human consciousness. Your body is like a temple and life is a gift from us Alien Gods. Mankind should strive for kindness, compassion, understanding, and equality. We left you thousands of ancient texts that all said the same thing: "Love thy neighbor as thyself." When you live by these words, intentional killing, anger and violence will dissipate from your planet and "Heaven on Earth 360" will be possible.

2. Stop creating deadly technology. Use technology in beneficial ways, not detrimental ways that harm humanity and the planet. Example: Tools for building, hunting and healing are good. Nuclear weapons, missiles and bombs designed to kill are evil. Deceptively, governments are trying to take away private gun rights; meanwhile, they harbor and create weapons trillions of times more powerful in the forms of nuclear bombs, missiles, tanks, battleships, and fighter jets. It's time *The People* start working together to control the government's deadly technologies. Humanity must 'Unite' and come together to agree to a complete and transparent *nuclear weapons disarmament* and plan to decommission battleships, submarines, tanks, fighter jets, missiles and bombs. Humans are the top species on Planet Earth. You are the Gods of Planet Earth and must promote living sustainably with Mother Nature. All the birds, bees, flowers and trees have no voice yet rely on Divine Men and Women to be their voice and advocate for them. Until mankind understands to use their powers and potential to create good for Planet Earth and care for Mother Nature, the planet will always be following the same chaotic wars, greed, destruction and hell on earth.

3. Create technology to help humanity and Mother Nature. Create technology that helps improve health and wellness of humans and Planet Earth. Release Tesla's free energy inventions we gave him a century ago. Humanity has many of these beautiful and planet saving technologies suppressed because *oil* companies have predicated on destroying any technology that would threaten their profits. *Power* and *energy* companies are also behind the suppression. Additionally, beer and liquor factories are examples of using technology to poison humanity and the environment. Once humanity is 'United' and comes together to promote healthy positive technologies, the planet will heal itself very quickly. Always remember: Cooperation>Competition.

4. Connect with Mother Nature more, human technology less. Connect with Mother Nature. She is the ultimate creator. When your planet was designed, we intentionally put plants, animals, and herbs to keep you healthy, happy, and heavenly. Pure human nature is to grow your own food and medicinal herbs because food and herbal medicine are the easiest and healthiest forms of healing. But now humans have abandoned the ancient healing remedies and come up with their own "cures" that are made in pharmaceutical labs, contaminated with poison all for corporate profits. Modern-day doctors are *indoctrinated* by corrupt corporations that prey off *The People*. Mother Nature says all plant medicine is 100% legal and for humans use. However, modern toxic 'elites' will often try to discredit Mother Nature/God. The original Declaration of Independence guaranteed each citizen Life, Liberty and Land. Owning land ensured that the citizens would have connection to plants, fungi, animals and Mother Nature. The planet can sustain its current population easily, if humans would *repopulate the land* *proportionately.* There are millions of acres of National Forest Lands that should be divvied up and given to *The People*, so they can reconnect with Mother Nature. But the slave-driven 40+ hour work week is an intentional overkill of spirit. Work weeks of ~25 hours/week are more in alignment with Mother Nature, allowing plenty of time to connect with family and self. Health is a simple recipe: every time you eat and put something in your mouth, it is only nutritious and nourishing food. The American food system is 90% processed and depleted foods; therefore, 90% of the people are getting sick. For thousands of years, humans understood and valued livestock. But now corporations have brain-washed humans to buy and sell 'dead-stock'. Please unite to reform the current technology-based corporate food and medical system. Positively, your bodies can heal themselves from positive thinking, rest/meditation, healthy foods, plant medicine, Yoga, warmth, and LOVE.

5. Fair taxes with reasonable wealth distribution. "Money is the root of all evil." Transparent taxes and fair wealth distribution sets the precedent for equality. Use technology to audit and ensure wealth has an honorable cap. For example, a collective society could place a wealth boundary cap of $1 billion. Nobody needs or should want more than $1 billion. This would inherently redistribute the wealth to more of humanity. Humans already have the technology available to make a 100% accountable finance and tax system. This is the ultimate way of helping ensure equality for society. Currently, a select handful of ultra-rich families have corroborated to divide the masses in every way possible, thereby inhibiting society from uniting and taking majority rule to enforce these morals, values and commandments. The dividing 'elite' wants to *brain-train* human minds to focus on everyone's differences and ignore the unifying practice of focusing on each other's similarities. Examples of division tactics, include feminism, LGBTQ-, race labeling, and two political party system. Humanity must 'Unite' on morals and values, unwavering. "When the power of love overcomes the love of power, the world will know peace." -Jimi Hendrix

6. Respect and promote family values. Mother and Father in household with children. There is undisputed scientific evidence that humans grow up and develop to become more healthy, confident, successful, happy and self-actualized when there is a Divine Mother and Divine Father in the household. Universally, there are **only 2** genders: Divine-Feminine and Divine-Masculine. Divine-Masculine: assertive, confident, energetic, wise, conservative, respectful, protective, strong morals, and caring. It's a centered Spirit that rests within 2 spectrums of a pendulum (see image). On one end of the spectrum, you have Aggressive-Toxic Masculine: lying, cheating, stealing, hardheaded, violent, unethical...lack of spiritual understanding. At the other end of the pendulum, you have Passive-Toxic Masculine: shy, quiet, people pleaser, too nice, passive-aggressive, anxious, insecure, etcetera. Then there is Divine Feminine: loving, kind, caring, understanding, supports her husband, respectful, motherly, strong healthy children, childbearing, nurturing, healing. Temptation drives the Aggressive-Toxic Feminine: manly, loud, controlling, angry, overly competitive, belittles men, no children by choice, antagonistic, sloppy. The other end of the spectrum, Passive-Toxic Feminine: Quiet, shy, too nice, doesn't know her worth, isolating, scared, timid, fearful, gullible, unsure, insecure. When both Divine parents are in the household, it creates an environment where there is always lots of love and balance. The Divine-Feminine does not pursue careers in the military, police, construction, politics or legal prosecutors as she understands this is Divine-Masculine's duty. However, she can have major influence through her vote and husband in these fields. Any other deviation from this model is a sin. LGBTQ-ideology conflicts with healthy family values. Let us explain. In society, in order for elders to retire, it's reliant on the previous generation's health, dependability, ethics, morals and values. Every couple(male-female) would need to be responsible for parenting 2 children for a steady replacement rate of humans. If parents do a really good job loving and raising their children, their kids will become wholesome and successful, thereby ensuring the senior generation's successful retirement. 'Divine Parenting' is the most important job in society and 'Until you're a parent, you're still a child'. For every selfish, childless 'gay couple' means Divine parents would need to have 4 kids, making their burden of responsibility unfairly heavier. Yet the children will have the

7

burden of caring/supporting the retired childless 'gay couple' who did not give their time, money or energy to the younger generation. Homosexuals will try to preach a lie that Love is *Love*. No, that is not true, because Sex between a man and woman creates *Life* and same-sex perversion creates demons. It is nowhere near the same. Anyone who has been wickedly encouraged to choose sexual perversion (LGBTQ-), can repent at any time and cross over to pure Divinity, Righteousness and Healing for your Spirit. Simply 'Make the Shift'. The best medicine we have provided to your planet to heal evil mind and spirit viruses is natural psychedelic medicine. Not man-made medicines!

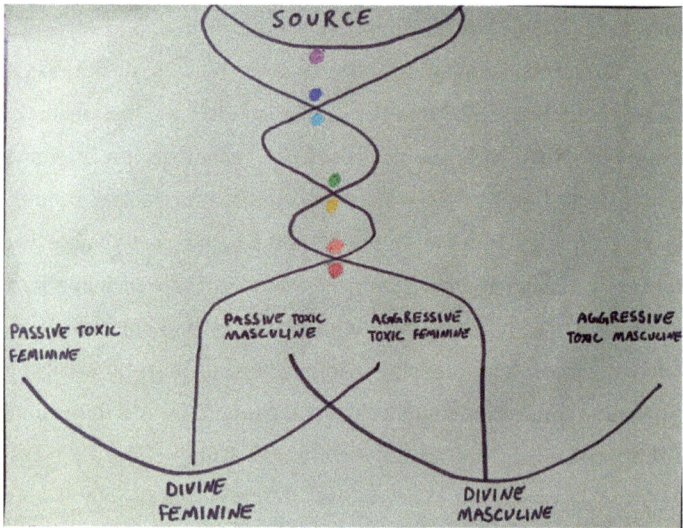

Rendition of image given by The Alien Gods.

7. Maintain 'Divine' Sex to Mother Nature connection.
Adult men and women are encouraged to have only Divine monogamous Sex. LGBTQ- is designed, funded and promoted by the corrupt ruling 'elite'. Homosexuality is a **choice** and most often the **result of suppressed trauma**. Mother Nature is about .0001% gay. Thank God, because if the plants and animals decided to be gay, everyone would starve. It takes a male and a female to create life. Yet why does 22% of college students 'identify' with LGBTQ-? Answer: LGBTQ- is intentional psychological manipulation. Telling people what's unnatural is natural and what's wrong is right. Basically, one giant *LIE*. Ironically, Gender Dysphoria (transgender) is listed in the DSM-5 as a mental health disorder. Then why would taxpayer-funded surgeons mutilate one's genitals? Give unnatural hormones? Praise the 'trans people' as brave? Answer: Because it makes medical corporations billions of dollars and divides/ weakens *The People* at the same time! The *dividing elite* and *mainstream media* promote single mothers as heroes, men as worthwhile workers, and mentally ill sexual perverts as 'exciting'. Truth be told, homosexuals are deprived of the spiritual crown of becoming a 'Father' or 'Mother'. The deceitful system named 'child support' is in reality a 'child neglect' system. Systemically incentivizing moms to break up the fatherly bond of the household. Additionally, Section 8 programs only provide housing if there is only 1 parent in the household and denies 2 parent families. Prostitution, paid sex and pornography are <u>completely unacceptable</u>. Divorce should

be the last option couples seek out. Everywhere else you look within other species on earth as well as the ancient texts we left you thousands of years ago point toward the importance of long-term monogamous marriage. Every man deserves a wife and every woman a husband, a 1:1 ratio. If someone is single, they are sinning, root word *sin*. Divine Feminine and Divine Masculine need each other to coexist. This helps heal the head of household (male), mother (female), children and society at large for generations. It's really that simple!

8. Practice Spiritual Health. Spirituality in a nutshell is practicing Gratitude: giving and receiving thanks and praise. The ritual of prayer before eating each meal is a gratitude practice and reminder. Also, speaking positive intentions into your food commands The Ether (5th element) to manifest one's desires. According to the law of synchronicity, states of consciousness such as Love, Peace, Joy, and Enlightenment are contagious to others. Similarly, fear, anger and guilt are also contagious to others. States of consciousness create vibration (see image). Nikola Tesla and Albert Einstein both referred to medicine of the future as simply vibration, sound and frequency. Positive thoughts and emotions create higher vibrations(vibes) in the body at an atomic level. Simply thinking positively will emit higher frequencies which help co-create 'Heaven on Earth 360". Religions are simply guides to spiritual health. Ceremonies such as singing in Church with large bells and organs were designed to help heal oneself and others simply through sound. (By the way, the Sabbath Day is Saturday, not Sunday.) The standard bowing prayer posture is the best stretch for the human spinal cord, a.k.a., the 'Tree of Life'. Semen retention raises a man's vibration. Every religion teaches about your God-self potential by activating your third-eye a.k.a. the pineal gland, a.k.a. 6th chakra. (Sadly though, fluoride is a neuro-toxin for the 6th chakra(brain). Humans have 7 chakras in total. The bottom three: root, sacral and solar plexus, are lower frequencies and where the toxic 'elites' want you to be stuck in. The top four chakras, heart, throat, third eye, and crown chakra are where you will find your higher God-self. Divine Feminine are naturally more gifted with the heart and crown chakra (green and purple) and Divine Masculine are more naturally gifted with their throat and third-eye chakra (light and dark blue). When Divine man and woman combine through spiritual marriage, they complement and maximize their magnificent potentials. However, inevitably with age the human body begins to decay, weaken and become less powerful. It's a common behavioral flaw that the elderly will be in denial of this fact and will try to retain powerful positions, when they should accept the *Truth* and pass the torch to the next generation.

Ultimately, humans' spiritual duty is to make the world a better *Palace* than they found it. They have a civic duty to themselves, ancestors, and descendants to ensure societies and governments operate within these 10 Commandments.

Map of Consciousness Levels

from David R. Hawkins *Power vs. Force*

700 -1000	ENLIGHTENMENT *Lord Buddha, Krishna, & Jesus Christ*	• Powerful inspiration • Attractor energy fields that influence all of mankind	
600	Saints, Healers, Advanced spiritually	PEACE	• Transcendence. God-consciousness • Great contributions to the world
540		JOY	• You have a notable effect on others • Individual will merges into divine will • Effortless / Synchronicity
Dissolves negativity 500		LOVE	• Purity of motive - from the heart • True happiness • Intuition
400		REASON	• Intelligence & rationality • Knowledge & education
350		ACCEPTANCE	• Major transformation - you are the source & creator of life
310		WILLINGNESS	• Success • Growth is rapid • Overcome inner resistance to life
250		NEUTRUALITY	• Energy becomes very positive • Beginning of inner confidence
Power first appears 200		COURAGE	• Level of Empowerment • Life is exciting
175		pride	• Dependant upon external conditions
150		anger	• Hate / Aggression - A moving energy
125		desire	• Greed / Insatiable
100		fear	• Worry & Anxiety
75		grief	• Sadness / Regret & Depression
50		apathy	• Helplessness / Hopeless
30		guilt	• Victimhood / Blame
20		shame	• Miserable / Humiliation

Creative Energy Expansion

Destructive Energy Contracted

NOTE: A person may operate on one level in any given area of life. An individuals overall level of consciousness is the sum total effect of all levels.

9. Keep children and adults truthful, innocent and pure hearted. Society shall honor, promote, and follow other humans that display these high morals, values and character. Look up to and reward people that are honest, ethical and pure hearted. Western societies are promoting toxic behavior with celebrities and politicians, thereby enticing the children and citizens with *evil*. When society honors and rewards good behavior and condemns bad behavior, it inherently creates an environment where humans will have incentive to do good. 'Trust creates Peace'. But toxic 'elites' like George Soros intentionally fund weak and immoral justice systems. Their intent is to not punish bad behavior; thereby, they encourage it and completely erode the fundamental Trust and Peace required for healthy societies.

10. Understand these Commandments came from God. Believe God is in each and every one of you. The *magic* of beliefs is *knowing* something to be true without seeing it. The etheric energy (5th Element) that holds the universe is invisible to the human eyeballs, thereby relies on *faith*. Air is also invisible to the human eyeballs, yet we all know it exists. God is not a mysterious man in the sky or any other statue or idol. Each and every human Being are Gods in disguise. Buddha, Jesus, Krishna and Mohammad all said the same thing. The moment you BELIEVE you are a God, and every other human is equally a *God* is when **Heaven on Earth 360** occurs. Your current governments are suppressing this once common information from humanity, because the corrupt leaders feed off domination, manipulation and control. The Shinto religion in Japan originates from *beings* in the *sky*. Similarly, the Holy Bible discusses angels in the sky in the book of Enoch. Unfortunately, the Vatican removed the book of Enoch from the Holy Bible centuries ago. Aliens are real! Angels are real! Spirits are real! And God is real!

PART 2

CURRENT DILEMMA IN SOCIETY (2024):

1% of the population controls 45% of the wealth. In modern society wealth means power which creates an oligarchy, and *The People* are forced to follow non-elected officials.

So what happens if humans deviate from the model provided by the Alien Gods?

Demons are created. Here are some examples:

- **Barack Obama** (Passive-Toxic Masculine/leader of LGBTQ-/woke ideology). His biological dad abandons him and creates a significant void in his soul. Children should be raised with a balance of Divine-Feminine and Divine-Masculine. In Obama's case he was deprived of Divine-Masculine energy, morals and values. And as a direct result with irreversible neurological damage, Obama grew into the Passive-Toxic Masculine. Simply put, *Obama was not raised right*. There was no masculine head of the household; he grew up in a dysfunctional matriarchy (i.e., femdom), and this is what he's comfortable with. He was sadly never taught how to responsibly use a hammer, shovel, firearms and most importantly his heart and brain. As Obama grew older and tried to fill the void that was a result of his father abandoning him, he searched for love from other men. Obama 'chose' homosexuality, and even went as low to pay homeless men for gay sex. "When a child is deprived of the love of both parents, they don't stop loving their parents; they stop loving themselves." Due to the self-hate buried deep into Obama's heart, he began to falsely blame America, white men and Christianity for his troubles caused by his unethical dad. Obama wanted to join the military but was denied, as the military did not accept homosexuality. But instead of manning up and correcting his flawed sexual perversion, Obama doubled down on his sins, and figured if he could legalize gay marriage, it would free his conscience. So in 2009, when the United States was engaged in *corrupt oil wars* and struggling through a *recession*, Obama took it upon himself to prioritize legalizing gay marriage? Make no mistake about it, Obama is a closet homosexual and promotes

LGBTQ- because 'Misery loves Company'. Ultimately Obama was elected primarily because of his skin color as America was sick and tired of being falsely accused of being a racist country. Good reason why humans should never allow flawed DEI/gender/race quotas which turned out to be a complete disaster. Later, in 2014 BLM (Black Lives Matter) riots became violent and claimed America was systemically racist. (Meanwhile there is a black president in their second term?) It provided a great opportunity for Obama to speak up against violence and remind people America once was racist but no longer was, as he is proof. But the Passive-Toxic Obama was nowhere to be found as he sat back and allowed BLM to create havoc and fuel racial division all over America. Later in 2014 Russia annexed Ukraine-Crimea and Obama's passive policies with his chosen secretary of state, Hillary Clinton, enabled Russia to invade Ukraine in 2022. Barack Obama admittedly is confused and insecure about his identity, as he wrote a book in 1995 about his personal struggles of being 50 percent black-50 percent white. He is openly the most racist man on earth, as evident by his movie he produced, *Leave the World Behind* (2023), when his script states: "Don't trust white people." Obama truly hates himself and America, as evident when he directed the removal of statues of America's white founding fathers, supported kneeling during the national anthem, and also condemned Edward Snowden, who blew the whistle that Obama's federal government was spying on their own citizens and infringing on civil liberties and constitutional rights. And the nail on the coffin for Obama's corruption is his net worth. Entering office with approximately $1 million and leaving with $70 million. Currently Obama is unethically and illegally working together with Joe Biden and Kamala Harris. Obama is committing borderline elder abuse by directing incompetent 'white' Biden to hire mentally ill, gay, trans, and people of color in the White House. Obama has also manipulated Biden to allow mentally ill trans people in the military. (Psst, Barack Obama is the Antichrist.) Furthermore, DEI (diversity, equity, and inclusion) is an extremely racist ideology. It encourages promotions based on their skin color and ignores human skills and qualifications. With DEI ideology, people with Down syndrome are underrepresented, Asians are underrepresented in professional sports, and children are underrepresented everywhere. And Barack Obama absolutely *killed his chef* because his chef knew without a doubt Michelle Obama is a transsexual *man*. But all Barack has to do is repent for his sins and cleanse his spirit. We left humans plant medicine and religions to heal your souls. "The

leaves of the tree were for the healing of the nations"
(Revelations 22:2).

• **Kamala Harris (Aggressive-Toxic Feminine).** Kamala
Harris's parents divorced when she was 7 years old, and
her mother 'won' full custody. This created a void in
Kamala because she was deprived of Divine Masculine
energy and thereby endured irreversible neurological
damage and developed into an Aggressive-Toxic
Feminine, a.k.a. man hater, a.k.a. daddy issues. She
would go on to believe men are adverse and all her
struggles are because America is sexist/racist. So
she went on a rampage to prove women are equal to
men and tried to prove her worth with her education
and career. However, when we look at her career,
it becomes very clear she is as toxic as it gets. Upon
graduating from a black college and law school, Kamala
Harris at the age of 29 began dating San Francisco
mayor Willie Brown, who was married and 61 years old.
She would then 'magically' get appointed to some high-
level political positions she was not qualified for, but
because she was having sex with a powerful political
figure. She would then continue screwing anyone in
her path to gain power. Kamala Harris as a prosecutor,
would convict countless men for cannabis possession,
wrecking the homes and livelihoods of many children.
And furthermore, once California legalized cannabis,

Kamala would fail to overturn her corrupt run of senseless convictions. Kamala Harris is as dirty, toxic and corrupt as a woman can get. It is also incredibly immoral to have a female such as Kamala commanding the military. She has no military experience, no parenting experience, and her entire career is built on screwing others for her personal gain.

"A woman should learn in quietness and full submission. I do not permit a woman to teach or to assume authority over a man; she must be quiet." (1 Timothy 2:11-12)

- **Bill Clinton (Passive-Toxic Masculine)** is a pedophile. **Hillary Clinton (Toxic-Aggressive Feminine)** is equally responsible, as she enabled him. Both their hands are not clean; there's lots of blood on them therefore belong in jail/hell. Remember Obama endorsed Hillary Clinton for president?

"Husbands and wives should satisfy each other's sexual desires. The wife does not have authority over her own body but yields it to her husband. In the same way, the husband does not have authority over his own body but yields it to his wife" (1 Corinthians 7:3-4).

- **Bill Gates (Passive-Toxic Masculine)** is also a pedophile. There is suppressed video evidence of him on Epstein Island. Once held accountable, all his wealth should be repossessed by The People and he should dwell in jail/

hell. This way he can be an example to other men why not to engage in pedophilia. Bill Gates is not thousands times smarter or more skilled than the average citizen, yet he has thousands times more wealth and power? "A perverse heart shall depart from me; I will know no evil" (Ps. 101:4).

- **Tulsi Gabbard (Aggressive-Toxic Feminine)**. Tulsi Gabbard is precisely what you do not want your daughters looking up to or following. Tulsi fully supports feminism, which is a divisive woke ideology built on a pyramid of lies which she is too blind to see. Thereby she views other men as competition instead of cooperation. From a young age Tulsi joined the US Army and has made a career out of it. She knows no better than the dirty, corrupt military industrial complex, which has been her primary source of income the entirety of her life. She also has been heavily involved in politics and has not done anything of consideration to fix the massive corruption schemes. The zodiac never lies, and Tulsi was born in the year 1982, which anoints her the 'Metal Rooster'. To no surprise she is very rigid and great at jacking her jaw; however, she lacks competence and any original independent free thinking. Thankfully she did not reproduce, so there will be no more Tulsi 'Haggard' genetics on the planet soon. Thereby Tulsi is not a mother and has no parenting experience but is the first one to tell other parents how to raise children. And to no surprise, she married a Passive-Toxic Masculine named Abraham Williams, who is basically the equivalent of a fruitcake mixed with a cornflake. Abraham has no backbone or courage and passively gives all his power away to Tulsi, who is pretending to be the man of the household. "For such people are not serving God, but their own appetites. By smooth talk and flattery they deceive the minds of naive people" (Romans 16:18).

- **Joe Biden (Aggressive-Toxic Masculine).** As many people know, a dog is a reflection of their owner. In the White House, Joe Biden's German shepherd dog has aggressively bitten dozens of innocent people. A telltale sign Joe has some unresolved anger buried within himself. And to no surprise, Joe Biden has started and fueled more wars in his tenure as president than anyone in recent history. Joe, who kept preaching "trust the science" in his corrupt push to get everyone vaccinated, is not following 'The Science'. There are countless studies that prove cognitive decline with age (see image). Joe is so far past his cognitive prime, he is *unfit for president*. Anyone past 75 years old should never become president, the most powerful job in the world. The US government mandates retirement at 64 years old for the military, mandates retirement for airline pilots at 67 and provides social security at 62. Because it is a widely known fact that with age, humans become less able. It makes no sense to have a president over 80 years old and give nuclear code decision-making to someone way past their cognitive prime. Lastly Joe Biden's son, who is also a reflection of Joe, is the least moral senator's son in recent history. Hunter Biden is a known drug addict, sex addict and shady businessman. Does it not seem fishy that Bidens were investigated for corruption in Ukraine in 2020, and now Biden is sending billions of dollars to Ukraine? Biden has been involved in government for 50+ years and had so many chances to fix corruption. He clearly is part of the deep state; he enables and supports weak values and morals. Military or blue-collar, honest, hard work is a prerequisite for good leaders.

Hard times create strong men. Strong men create good times. Good times create weak men. And, weak men create hard times.

—G. Michael Hopf,

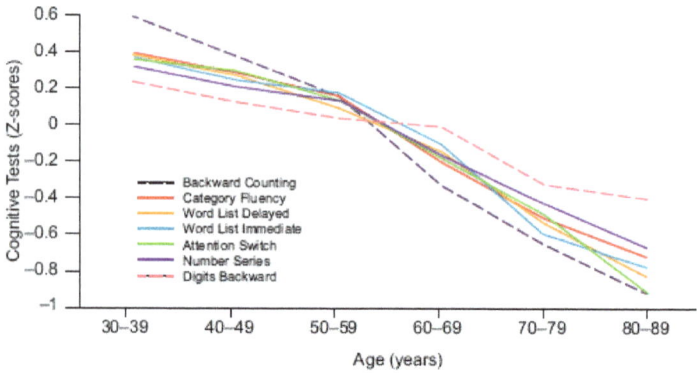

Scientific study proving significant cognitive decline with age.

- **Donald Trump (Aggressive-Toxic Masculine).** Trump is not much better than Biden. If Trump is elected, he would be the oldest president ever, even older than Biden. This would be a huge mistake, as *The People* would be giving the most powerful job in the world to someone who is absolutely cognitively impaired. A very common mistake elders make is not passing the torch when they exit their prime. If Trump did such a great job raising his children, then he should give his business, politics and legacy to his sons. But Trump's selfish EGO (edging God out) is in denial and can't accept the cold, hard *Truth*. There is no substitute to experience and simply Trump has no experience working a blue-collar job and cannot relate to the average American citizen. Trump was handed a silver spoon and born into extraordinary wealth. And if Trump was a great president, he should have eliminated the deep state during his 4 years of presidency. He had his shot; he missed his chance. Trump needs to let go of his ego, endorse someone younger than him, go happily *retire* and play golf.

Basically, the whole Democratic party and Hollywood are bought, toxic and corrupt. Democrats have had control of the US federal government for 12 of the last 16 years and let's look at how screwed up they've made things. The military industrial complex has grown tremendously under their rule, as evident by the billions of dollars they have spent on foreign wars. They conduct a medical system that prescribes children a known neuro-toxin pill called fluoride and mutilate childrens genitals. They fund and support all Psychological Operations (feminism, LGBTQ-, racial division, gender theory, etcetera). They support lawlessness, as evident by the southern border, and also institute backward laws, such as listing cannabis as an illegal felony (a schedule 1 drug), while a large majority of the states have *contradictory* cannabis laws. The democratic leaders are completely bought and sold by the major corporations and families, such as the Rockefellers, Blackrock, Vanguard, Rothschilds, Gates, etcetera. Gavin Newsom is also possessed by demons. And Klaus Schwab is a mass manipulator. None of the current Democratic party leaders can be trusted nor followed.

P.S. The terror attack Hamas supposedly surprise attacked Israel on October 7, 2023, was a 'false flag' operation very similar to 9/11. Israel attacked themselves. Israel claimed about '1200' citizens died. By use of deception, Israel self-created a 'reason' to invade Gaza. Mysteriously, Israel has gained US support to invade and steal Palestinian land. Why? Because MOSSAD (Israel's CIA) had hidden cameras on Epstein Island and blackmailed the United States to support Israel's petty war, or Israel would release video evidence of US senators, congressmen and celebrities committing pedophilia. Israel is committing genocide as evident by the 36,000+ dead civilians compared to '1200' dead Israelis. Israel is more atrocious than Russia. Russia hasn't killed nearly as many innocent men, women, and children in 2.5 years as Israel had in 2 months! Within Israel's religious Holy Book, the Sixth Commandment forbids intentional killing as gravely sinful yet gives permission for an eye for an eye. Israel is being completely hypocritical and in defiance of all Religions. The world goes to hell when world leaders like Biden, Obama, and Kamala Harris remain in power. Humans must 'Make the Shift'. Divine Men and Women create a Divine World and toxic men and women create a toxic world.

If you are starting to feel sick because you now know how disastrous and perverted the deep state is, that is very normal. However, hang in there. The solutions to these problems are coming up.

- **Robert F. Kennedy Jr. (Divine Masculine).** He is the Savior and Answer to fix the deep state corruption. Robert F. Kennedy has an amazing track record of fighting corrupt corporations during his career as an environmental lawyer. He is not bought and sold by any corporations and displays Divine morals and values within these 10 Commandments. He is running for president as an Independent. If elected, he would work hard to unite *The People* and fight the common enemy (corrupt corporations and politicians). We Alien Gods are wishfully asking *The People* to Wake-up, Unite and Vote Independent Robert F. Kennedy. This will be the start of Heaven on Earth 360.

- **Cheryl Hines (Divine Feminine).** Now that you are an expert in these concepts and utilizing your intuition... what do you see when you look into Cheryl's eyes? Eyes are the gate-way and portal to the soul. Cheryl's eyes and soul exhibit a delicate balance of an angel and sweet nurturing mother with a pure heart. She perfectly balances her husband, Robert F. Kennedy Jr., and is so deserving to become the First Lady of the United States of America.

POEMS TO CELEBRATE FINISHING THE BOOK!

From the writer Rion Baxter (Divine Masculine): I have never been a poet or a writer, but that all changed one day when a good friend of mine gave me a Magic Mushroom chocolate bar. I ate the chocolate bar unknowing of the Divine Power and Medicine it contained. I used to suffer from lots of anxiety and depression, but the natural plant medicine Healed my Soul. I give Thanks and Praise to Mother Nature and Father God for teaching me how to embody my Divine Masculine Nature.

THE MEDICINE MANJA

A Poem Written by Rion Baxter

First it was the wild grass, it couldn't be tamed but then we learned a new way—machinery,

Then it was the wild pigs, they couldn't be tamed, then we learned a new way, snares and weaponry,

Then it was the wild sheep, they couldn't be tamed, but then we learned fences and boundaries,

Then it was the spirits they couldn't be tamed, then we...

The chicken starts screaming, I threw her some food, the peace ensued,

The goat began pulling, a struggle it was, I threw her some food, the peace ensued,

The cat began to whine, loudly we heard, I placed a bowl of food, the peace ensued,

The dog began tearing into trash, a mess it was, I gave some old chicken bones, the peace ensued.

The stomach began to claw and scratch, the pain was real, I gave her some food, the peace ensued.

The thieves began to creep at night, scary it was, we placed a basket of food, the peace ensued.

The villagers began to rumble and light things on fire, the community leader offered food, the peace ensued.

Society figures out abundance of food is great, the more food the merrier nature agrees.

But then diseases ramped up in all species worldwide, the leaders gave them food, but so many still died.

They kept throwing food, like the doctrine prescribes, someone said, 'Hey, when we give food no longer does peace ensue.'

A medicine man from the woods claimed the food is now poop, we must revert to our roots.

They called him a caveman and shunned him to exile. He agreed that's fine and said, 'You will see in a while.'

The problems got worse and no one could find the right solutions, so again in time,

They circled and circled and looked to 'the science', finally a scientist spoke in defiance.

He said, 'The science says we must go back to food ways that we once had.'

He claims the ultimate scientist was Mother Nature, her we should listen to most, not other people.

The people began to understand, and slowly settled with less, and so many began to get out of that mess,

More and more began to listen to Mother Nature, it was like she was their Creator.

Then all of a sudden, a village was found, a medicine man was glowing in the sand.

A lake of gold and pyramid of stone, that no one was prepared to own,

The next newest truth he cried with glee, is that Mother Nature is ruled by the Holy,

People again asked how could he question, the ultimate scientist Mother Nature,

He said, 'I don't question but come with proof- aliens exist. I called them Gods of Good,'

They laughed and joked and said he was stoned, back he went to exile, but he went with a smile.

The peaceful years ensued and that was great, until enough people began to frustrate.

They claimed to see spirits and lights in the sky, the people yelled, 'Government come out of disguise!'

The government didn't have the answers and people feared hard, 'What are these things flying in our yards?'

Then finally one official decided to unseal...what he believed was the real deal.

'The Universe' he said 'has all our answers, just send up your message, and it will answer your prayer.'

People began to buy in and the earth began to glow, next thing you know they could produce gold,

Then one day appeared something old, it was the medicine man, but as a glowing orb.

He kissed each being's forehead and wished them good night, but the time had come for him to take flight.

A flash and a bang the planet's food he would anoint, the Gardens of Eden rested her first night.

And as always, the cycle of the universe...continues its morph...

With Love,
+Rion Baxter

THOSE WHO REMAIN
A Poem Written by Martin Niemöller

First they came for the Socialists, and I did not speak out—Because I was not a Socialist.

Then they came for the Trade Unionists, and I did not speak out—Because I was not a Trade Unionist.

Then they came for the Jews, and I did not speak out—Because I was not a Jew.

Then they came for me—and there was no one left to speak for me.

A S   I   B E G A N   T O   L O V E   M Y S E L F
A Poem Written by Kim McMillen

As I began to love myself
I found that anguish and emotional suffering
are only warning signs that I was living
against my own truth.
Today, I know, this is **Authenticity.**

As I began to love myself
I understood how much it can offend somebody
if I try to force my desires on this person,
even though I knew the time was not right
and the person was not ready for it,
and even though this person was me.
Today I call this **Respect.**

As I began to love myself
I stopped craving for a different life,
and I could see that everything
that surrounded me
was inviting me to grow.
Today I call this **Maturity.**

As I began to love myself
I understood that at any circumstance,
I am in the right place at the right time,
and everything happens at the exactly right moment.
So I could be calm.
Today I call this **Self-Confidence.**

As I began to love myself
I quit stealing my own time,
and I stopped designing huge projects
for the future.
Today, I only do what brings me joy and happiness,
things I love to do and that make my heart cheer,
and I do them in my own way
and in my own rhythm.
Today I call this **Simplicity.**

As I began to love myself
I freed myself of anything
that is no good for my health—
food, people, things, situations,
and everything that drew me down
and away from myself.
At first I called this attitude a healthy egoism.
Today I know it is **Love of Oneself.**

As I began to love myself
I quit trying to always be right,
and ever since
I was wrong less of the time.
Today I discovered that is **Modesty.**

As I began to love myself
I refused to go on living in the past
and worrying about the future.
Now, I only live for the moment,
where everything is happening.
Today I live each day,
day by day,
and I call it **Fulfillment.**

As I began to love myself
I recognized
that my mind can disturb me
and it can make me sick.
But as I connected it to my heart,
my mind became a valuable ally.
Today I call this connection **Wisdom of the Heart.**

We no longer need to fear arguments,

confrontations or any kind of problems

with ourselves or others.

Even stars collide,

and out of their crashing, new worlds are born.

Today I know: **This is Life!**

FINAL RECAP

The whole Democrat "woke agenda" is a calculated NWO plan to weaken the masses. Anytime corporations and governments are *forcing* ideas, that's a giant red-flag. There have been countless instances of the Democrat Party blatantly lying. They ruined their own credibility. Like when the Democrats/vaccine companies told everyone the vaccine was harmless. It was harmful, made the 'elites' billions and made *The People* sick at the same time.

Please Wake up, Unite, and overturn all these sick, perverted leaders. 'United we stand, divided we fall'. Escape the two-party trap; Vote for a third party such as Independent! This will open the door to a 4th and 5th Party thereby giving *The People* better selection and choices in their policy leaders.

Plant medicine for everyone! Peyote, mushrooms, ayahuasca for all, cannabis for all, edible healing herbal gardens for all! Mother Nature has everything you need.

We kindly ask for humanity to live righteously with morals and values within these 10 Commandments. 'Make the Shift' Honor the ancient texts and religious teaching we have given your planet to create 'Heaven on Earth 360'. Or humanity can continue on their current timeline of destruction, greed, pain, death and perpetual 'hell on earth'. If you don't study history/religion, it keeps repeating itself (e.g. Sodom and Gomorrah).

Simplified: If you are a female, you strive to perfect your Divine Feminine. If you are a male, you strive to perfect your Divine Masculine, a.k.a. highest-self, a.k.a. God. Make no mistake about it, men and women have very different roles but are equally dependent on each other.

LAST RE-MINDER

Planet Earth's problem: Man-made corporate matrix with collaboration of the corrupt Democrat and Republican Party (e.g., food, oil, military, medical, financial corporations).

The solutions: Shop local, move out of the cities, populate with nature.

Make Love, Make babies. Stay loyal. Do your best! Enjoy life. Live with Mother Nature. 'Make the Shift' #wakeup #speakup #standup. Reform the corrupt corporations/governments. Align and tune in with your spiritual essence. This is the dream of Heaven on Earth 360.

Hallelujah and Mahalo!
IG: @heaven.on.earth360 provider,healer.

ENCORE/ UPDATE: MAY 17TH 2024

Never-ever let anyone tell you: you're too small to make a difference. The book 'The Alien Gods: 10 Commandments' manuscript was written and submitted to publisher on March 11th 2024. Mysteriously a huge slew of social topics discussed in the book have been changed by the Demon Rat Party leaders. We knew the deep state was full of crooks, but never thought they would go this low as to steal a sovereign beings writings, take all the solutions and 'pretend to be their own', and then pass an law which the author cannot publish the book or receive any profits from his meticulous works (illegal and unconstitutional)? Without a doubt my laptop was hacked and my propriety information and content was stolen by MOSSAD, then given to the White House. However, the firewall was intentionally left open by US tech companies/AIPAC. If the Demon Rat Party truly cared about its citizens, they would have made these changes in year 1. Not 3.5 years into their rule, in a desperate attempt to win re-election. We'll let you be the judge, but here are the facts. All these issues are discussed in the '43 page' short book...All of a sudden, Biden has proposed laws banning toxic food ingredients? DEI (diversity, equity, inclusion) is now all of a sudden been 'renamed'? Prostitutes have been added to LGBTQ- in attempt to gain strength in numbers for the 'sexual immoral club'(LGBTQ-)? Marijuana was reclassified from schedule 1 drug to schedule 3 drug? Vaccine companies are suddenly admitting negative side effects? US Army is running commercials advertising recruitment into their Psychological Operations Division*. The Anti-semitism ACT was passed and signed into law which forbids criticizing the WAR in ISRAEL(~May 20th). Hypocritically Demon Rats were criticizing Russia for passing a law forbidding criticizing the war in Russia? The law is 100% unconstitutional and mesmerizing 535+ members of congress who have one purpose **Do not screw up the constitution or bill of rights**, and then they proceed to infringe on citizens first amendment right. This is blatant proof BOTH parties are bought and sold! The Demon Rat Party hosted a private party at the 'Black House' where they invited all the top social media stars and have requested them to start pushing ANTI-RELIGION PROPOGANDA/BUT PRO JOE BIDEN? Chem-trails used to be a 'conspiracy theory' but now is a widely known fact. And additionally, May 17th THE POPE of the Vatican held a Press conference regarding ALIENS and setting protocols, he is the only one who can validate any claims with ALIENS??? Peacock Television is set to release a bogus nature film on animal sexuality on 6/6? George Soros publicly admitted recently to financing a multi-billion dollar censorship program? And the Federal government is Tracking Holy Bible sales? Suppressed Free-energy technology has been released? Last but not least, I have also received death threats if I publish the book...hmm must be some pretty good stuff in the manuscript the Demon Rats don't want getting out? (I am highly trained and skilled in remote viewing and have received lots of information via this technique. Ironically Google just removed the video that teaches about remote viewing..?)

Additional information: Balak Obama is 100% the Anti-Christ. Revelations 2:14 discusses the Anti-Christ as person named Balak with last name Balaam who will set up Israel, feed everyone poisonous foods and promote sexual immorality. Homosexuality and all Sexuality is 100% a choice. We are responsible for our choices and actions. However, what was not Balak's fault was his childhood. He was created during immoral sexual prostitution. And then born into the home of a single prostitute mother. Early in Balak's childhood he would have to witness and hear countless random men having sex with his mother in exchange for money. And to no surprise Balak's childhood was also sold into pedophile prostitution. As you can imagine, being a child such as Balak and not choosing the environment. But nevertheless, that does not permit Balak to continue the pattern and force it upon other children's lives. He may have an excuse 'its okay, this is how I was raised, and I end up being President! Its good for children to be sexually active with adult men at a young age!'... Divine Sex is the stem/root/result of every single human on earth. However, if done immorally, it will create negative connections with each other's soul who partook in the 'unholy' act. Only Balak knows his exact body count, but there are lots of intertwined souls stemming back to the very simple question. Marriage/Sex is only between God given birth assigned gender of a 1 man and 1 woman? Strangely Chuck Schumer wife was born a man, and he is connected deeply with Israel? If you have noticed the world and societies have rapidly become very negative/corrupt. Some will blame it on cell phones, but when you look deeper you see it all about sexual morality. That is the premise of a healthy society. Once sexual morals start slipping, it creates a never-ending slope of what acceptable sexually and what's not. And lastly if I was a 62-year-old homosexual who loved having sex with 18-year-old boys, I would try everything in my power to brainwash everyone to spread their ass cheeks for my pool/selection/liking. The more the merrier, right? As a straight heterosexual male, I have noticed dating women the last few years has become extraordinarily peculiar. A lot of sexual confusion, darkness, looseness, tightness, and erratic beliefs in general regarding sexual morals. Its like everyone is all over the map and no one knows what is Right and what's wrong.

Weirdos like Bill Gates want de-population and LGBTQ- is his best friend and he is vehemently trying to defend the flawed belief system... Anyways you get the drift, and we are adamant about fixing the minds, innocence and pure-heartedness of our youth and future generations to come. Feel free to follow us on IG : heaven.on.earth360 X/twitter: JesusChrist2030

In anticipation of Gay Pride Month...We are hopeful we can get ahead of this one and stop the demonic timeline. The Demon Rat Party and AIPAC/Jews/Israel are planning a false flag terrorist attack worldwide. The plan is to have Muslim migrants cause violence at gay/LGBTQ- pride parades. Then after the world see's the Muslims as evil, Israel will nuke Iran. Again, hopeful this doesn't happen. Revelations 2:14 "But I have a few things against you, because you have there those who hold the doctrine of Balaam, who taught Balak to put a stumbling block before the children of Israel, to eat things sacrificed to idols, and to commit sexual immorality." Revelations 13:18 "Here is wisdom. Let him who has understanding calculate the number of the beast, for it is the number of a man: His number is 666." Lots of sexual immorality and a mysterious quest for someone to identify the 666 mark of the beast. Coincidentally the LGBTQ- flag is a FALSE rainbow with 6 stripes? A REAL rainbow has 7 colors! ROYGBIV, red, orange, yellow, green, blue, indigo, violet = 7. LGBTQ+ = 6! And the whole 'club' is about S-E-X-U-A-L=6! M-O-R-A-L-S=6! V-A-L-U-E-S=6! B-A-R-A-C-K=6! K-A-M-A-L-A=6! Ironically the flaggy rainbow club is 100% about sexual immorality! However, if you know your Religious texts, you come to realize that Marijuana and Mushrooms are 100% Legal if used for Spiritual Enlightenment purposes in accordance with the Holy Bible as protected by THE FIRST AMMENDEMENT OF THE UNITED STATES OF AMERICA, FREEDOM OF SPEECH AND FREEDOM OF RELIGION SHALL NOT BE INFRINGED. We would never expose a problem without the THE SOLUTION. First off, there is ONE RACE, The Human Race. All humans are different shades of brown. No one is white or black, those are divisive lies! Secondly, A NEW FLAG that does represents a UNITED WORLD. It's inspired from Bob Marley and called O-N-E L-O-V-E =7 represents M-O-T-H-E-R-S=7 F-A-T-H-E-R-S=7 C-H-A-K-R-A-S=7 R-O-Y-G-B-I-V=7. 7 points to the Mary Jane leaf. The 7th charkra is the most powerful and represents spirit, however old jew religion DENIES this truth so hard they wear black caps on their head to block out the 7th chakra. The NEW FLAG is a REAL R-A-I-N-B-O-W=7 that has purple on the top just like our 7th chakras. Unlike the FAKE rainbow flag that has red on top, which is your root chakra/butthole, and to no surprise they think with their butthole first. LGBTQ- A contagious neurological flawed belief system that is very resistant to change. The 'scientific' brain scans show blood flow only to the lower regions of the brain; hence they are stuck in 'heel/hell'. The Awakened/ Enlightened Beings must encourage them to take their plant medicine and RISE with the rest of us to co-create Heaven on Earth 360! And with that said, Jesus Christ agrees! Jesus Christ is simply a mindset of

Peace and Love! He and his 12 hippie disciple friends got sick of Babylon city and went out into the forest to retreat. However, they discovered MARY JANE and hence were born from the 'Virgin Mary'. They also found Magic Mushrooms and got super happy and smart from them! They wrote the New Testament and declared themselves NEW JEWS. They returned to the city to teach the people that Weed and Mushrooms can heal everyone and the OLD JEWS got mad and chastised Jesus and his hippie disciple friends. So here we are on the verge of the NEW GOLDEN AGE 2030 and Christ has re-risen! Yes, the movement is here of Jesus Christ's TRUE message of all nations needing cannabis and magic mushrooms to heal. The current problems on earth are so deeply intertwined and messy, that the only real solution to Global Peace and Love is widespread Cannabis and Mushrooms which will lead to a lovely NEW EARTH!

With that said here are some religious verses that Governments/ Oligarchs don't want you knowing. Revelations 2:7 "Whoever has ears, let them hear what the Spirit says to the churches. To the one who is victorious, I will give the right to eat from the tree of life, which is in the paradise of God." Isaiah 31:11 "and the anointing oil and fragrant incense for the Holy Place. They are to make them just as I commanded you." Genesis 1:29 "So God said, "Behold, I have given you every plant yielding seed that is on the surface of the entire earth, and every tree which has fruit yielding seed; it shall be food for you." For more info: www. thc-ministry.org

Ultimately, after taking the time to study the communist playbook, the college students are the ONES! Yes Blow-bama and friends are mimicking 'Communist Tyrannical Dictator Mao/Stalin'. For instance, in April 2024, the demon rats enticed college students to protest the war they created in Gaza? Utilizing blatant lies in a protest handbook, that was developed, funded and printed by the deep-state. Forcing completely flawed ideologies such as 'racial injustice' 'transphobia' 'gender theory'. Upon using the college students as pawns, the demon rats turned around, used the protest against all citizens and proceeded to pass a law stripping and infringing on the first amendment and freedom of speech. If anyone is promoting gender theory, they are completely full of shit! Luckily if you are a college student, this is the biggest election in the history of the world and it largely starts with YOU! The current system is planning on trapping everyone into a cashless, mindless and controlled society. However, by utilizing natural psychedelic plant medicine, the expansion of human consciousness will create a world of love, which cannot be controlled. "They fear love because it creates a world they can't control."
George Orwell, 1984

(Disclaimer: Anyone who is considering a surgical sex change operation, we highly encourage you take some Magic Mushrooms

FIRST! Yes, the little things growing all over the world that look exactly like a penis. Mother Nature's spirit-sex medicine. And some recommended music artists to listen to are: #1 Bob Marley #2 SOJA #3 60's & 70's Psychedelic Rock. Jah Bless   )

Milton Keynes UK
Ingram Content Group UK Ltd.
UKHW050858220724
445793UK00007B/17

9 798822 947160